# SPIRITUAL STRATEGIES

TO COMBAT BARRENNESS IN RELATION TO THE WOMB

Chiduzie Nmecha

**Spiritual Strategies to Combat Barrenness**

# SPIRITUAL STRATEGIES *to* COMBAT BARRENNESS *in* RELATION TO THE WOMB.

CHIDUZIE NMECHA

## ABOUT THE BOOK

The book came about by the leading of the Holy Ghost. I have spent the best part of over 20 years praying for couples, believing God for the fruit of the womb. The years of experience of praying with couples, listening to the challenges they have encountered whilst waiting on the Lord, has enabled me put together the various strategic keys to combat barrenness: such as the need of revelational knowledge, the power of the spoken word, the role of evil altars, dismantling the role of witchcraft, dealing with evil weapons, uprooting evil plantation and deliverance from spiritual prisons. This Book, by the Grace of God, is to reach its target audience, especially those who are trusting and believing God for the fruit of the womb. This book has a section on testimonies, which proves that God is still in the business of answering prayers and increasing one's faith.

# Spiritual Strategies to Combat Barrenness

This study is a summary of years of teaching, praying and intercession for couples struggling to conceive. This book can be used during prayer. It can also be used during study groups and personal study.

© Chiduzie Nmecha 2025

**All rights reserved.**

For questions and enquiries: email: Chiduzienm@gmail.com

No part of this publication may be reproduced or transmitted in any form or by means, electronic or mechanical, including photocopying, recording or any other storage and retrieval system without permission in writing from the Author.

Spiritual Strategies to Combat Barrenness

# Table of Contents

**APPRECIATION** 7

**INTRODUCTION** 8

**CHAPTER ONE**
  Importance of Revelation 12
  Prayer Points 15

**CHAPTER TWO**
  The Role of the Spoken Word 16
  Prayers: Dealing with Evil/Strange Words/Evil Decrees 19

**CHAPTER THREE**
  The Role of Evil Altars 22
  Prayers to Destroy Evil Altars 25

**CHAPTER FOUR**
  Dismantling the Role of Witchcraft 28
  Prayers: Dismantling Witchcraft Powers 30

**CHAPTER FIVE**
  Dealing with Evil Weapons. 32
  Prayers: Dealing with Evil Weapons 33

**CHAPTER SIX**
  Uprooting Evil Plantations. 36
  Prayers to Uproot Evil Plantations 38

**CHAPTER SEVEN**
  Deliverance From Spiritual Prisons 42
  How to Get Out of the Spiritual Prison 45
  Deliverance Prayers From Spiritual Prisons 46

**TESTIMONIES** 50

# APPRECIATION

I would like to thank God Almighty for the inspiration to put this book together for His glory.

I would like to thank my family for the surprise they had when they discovered I was writing a book. This book was not something planned. It came by the inspiration of the Holy Ghost.

I would like to thank friends whom I shared the revelation with about writing a book, they encouraged me immensely, I bless God for all the well-wishers, and all those who made time to write their testimonies, included in this book.

# INTRODUCTION

According to the Scripture in Genesis 1:26-28 especially verse 28, it states, "And God blessed them, and God said unto them be fruitful and multiply and replenish the earth and subdue it: and have dominion over the fish and the sea, and over the fowl of the air, and over every living thing that move upon the earth."

Looking at the Scripture, it is the will of God for couples to have children, however the enemy has introduced barrenness. According to the Scripture in John 10:10, "The thief cometh not, but for to steal, and to kill, and to destroy: The original plan of God, from the beginning, was for man to be **fruitful** as stated in the word of God, however the enemy has his three-fold ministry to **steal**, **kill** and to **destroy**. Barrenness can be defined as the inability for a woman to conceive or have children.

There are various strategies the enemy uses to introduce barrenness into the life of a woman, so she cannot conceive: like the woman having repeated miscarriages. By the Grace of God, I went to minister deliverance some many years ago, and that day, there was a minister that assisted me to minister. All of a sudden, the Lord gave me a word (she would get pregnant). I gave the minister that assisted me the prophecy the Lord gave me. The minister said it could never happen, because she had been through over thirty miscarriages, and these were the miscarriages that she could even remember. To the glory of the Living God, she carried the pregnancy full term and delivered safely.

There is another couple, who the wife had miscarriages, and have agreed to write their testimony, which will be in the testimony section of this book.

I would like to thank those who have written testimonies. These testimonies will be shared in the testimony section.

Another weapon the enemy uses to bring about barrenness is constant quarrelling between spouses. One of the testifiers, who God has now blessed with a child, was always quarrelling at the appointed time of conception. I bless God for the Pastor has written a testimony, which is in the testimony section of the book.

In this Book, one will examine the various strategies of how to deal with barrenness. Strategy can be defined as a way of diagnosing a problem, such as barrenness. How it can be solved; the set of several ways it can be addressed, by using the word of God. Also, identifying various prayer topics which will deliver one from barrenness in Jesus' name. Barrenness is a weapon the devil uses to afflict homes, breaking up homes and marriages, which sometimes leads the man into polygamy.

The ministry of the fruit of the womb is very dear to my heart, from a personal and family point of view. When our son was born, twenty-six years ago, we were informed by the medical team at the Hospital that he would never talk, never walk and that he would be in a wheelchair for life. To the glory of God, we stood on the word of God and engaged in prayer. Today, the young man is talking, walking, plays football and is an Usher in the church. The spiritual battle we faced during the pregnancy for our son, equipped one for the next pregnancy. The birth of our daughter. The Almighty God has prepared and equipped one on how to pray and support those seeking the fruit of the womb.

The strategic keys to combat barrenness, listed below, will be discussed within the chapters of this book.

1. The role of the Power of Revelation.
2. The role of the Spoken Word.
3. The role of Evil Altars.
4. Dismantling the role of Witchcraft.
5. Dealing with Evil Weapons.
6. Uprooting Evil Plantations.
7. Deliverance from Spiritual Prisons.
8. Testimonies.

**Spiritual Strategies to Combat Barrenness**

# CHAPTER ONE

## THE IMPORTANCE OF REVELATION

According to the Scripture Hosea 4:6, "My people are destroyed for lack of knowledge: because thou has rejected knowledge, I will also reject thee, that thou shalt be no priest to me, seeing thou hast forgotten the law of thy God, I will also forget thy children."

Revelation or divine revelation is a way of disclosing some form of truth or knowledge through communication with a deity. We need revelation from the Living God concerning issues that arise in our lives.

According to the scripture in 2nd Timothy 2:15, "Study to shew thyself approved unto God, a workman that needed not to be ashamed, rightly dividing the word of truth." This scripture is relevant in the context of truth.

1. Look at your Generation.
2. Are their family patterns from father's side of the family?
3. Are their family patterns from mother's side of the family?
4. In terms of conception are there any patterns of delay, miscarriages, still birth from both sides of the family.

If one went to see a doctor concerning Blood Pressure, Glaucoma, Diabetes, the Doctor would want to ascertain whether there was any history of such conditions in the family before giving a diagnosis. I met a Medical Doctor at my workplace who came to pick up his medication for blood pressure. I said to the Doctor, "you are forty years old, why are you taking medication for blood pressure?" He answered and said, "it is hereditary."

This is why we need revelational knowledge from God to ensure the right prayers are done.

According to the scripture in John 8:32, "And ye shall know the truth and the truth shall make you free." As a young man growing up, I discovered that six men died prematurely in my family, they were all under fifty years old, not married and did not have any children. By the time I gave my life to Christ, I knew I had to pray that every curse of untimely death, programmed into my generation, break by fire and be powerless against me.

In the context of barrenness affecting couples with the inability to conceive. Here are some effective prayers:

1. Lord reveal to me the secret behind the problem.
2. Lord expose every secret in my generation that is responsible for barrenness.
3. Lord reveal every secret of my father's house that is responsible for barrenness.
4. Lord reveal every secret of my mother's house that is responsible for barrenness.
5. Lord reveal the secret of my in-laws that is responsible for barrenness.
6. Lord reveal to me secrets of past relationships that are responsible for barrenness.

According to scripture, Psalm 62:11 says, "God hath spoken once, twice have I heard that power belongeth unto God. God is faithful when you seek His face concerning the Fruit of the Womb. When God begins to show you the secret behind why one is barren, why one has not conceived, you will need wisdom to manage the revelation from God. There are two instances I want to refer to in the Bible. In Genesis 37, the Bible tells us that Joseph had a dream and told his brethren. The Bible says Joseph's brethren hated him for his dreams and his words. They conspired to slay him and said we shall see what will become of his dreams. Look at Matthew 2, concerning the birth of Our Lord Jesus Christ.

13 "And when they were departed, behold, the angel of the Lord appeared to Joseph in a dream, saying, Arise, and take the young child and his mother, and flee into Egypt, and be thou there until I bring thee word: for Herod will seek the young child to destroy him.

14 When he arose, he took the young child and his mother by night, and departed into Egypt:

15 And was there until the death of Herod: that it might be fulfilled which was spoken of the Lord by the prophet, saying, Out of Egypt have I called my son.

16 Then Herod, when he saw that he was mocked of the wise men, was exceeding wroth, and sent forth, and slew all the children that were in Bethlehem, and in all the coasts thereof, from two years old and under, according to the time which he had diligently inquired of the wise men."

The lesson in the second story is that Joseph took Jesus and Mary away at night, he never discussed it with anybody, here, wisdom was applied. When God is revealing the secret behind a problem, don't make a mistake and begin to tell everyone, like Joseph did in Genesis 37. This will empower the enemy to continue in wickedness.

### Prayer Points:

1. Father God, baptise me with wisdom.
2. Father God, release your grace upon my life, so that I do not expose myself to the enemy.
3. Father God, release your grace for me, so that I walk in your truth.
4. Father God, release your grace to abide in your truth.
5. Father God, release your grace for me to control my mouth.
6. Father God, release your grace to obey divine instructions.
7. Father God, give me the heart to believe your word.
8. Powers sitting upon my gift of revelation, be unseated by fire.
9. Powers blocking my divine communication with God, be challenged by fire.
10. Blood of Jesus purge my spiritual pipe.
11. Every blockage in my spiritual pipe, be consumed by fire.

# CHAPTER TWO

## THE ROLE OF THE SPOKEN WORD

Words are powerful, words can make and can destroy. It is important to be careful of the words we speak concerning our life, destiny, marriage, and children.

Let's look at the following scriptures:

(1) Genesis 1:3 "And God said let there be light: and there was light."
(2) Genesis 1:26 "And God said, let us make man in our image, after our likeness: and let them have dominion over the fish of the sea, and over the fowl of the air, and over the cattle, and over all the earth, and over every creeping thing that creepeth upon the earth.
(3) Genesis 1:27) "So God created man in his own image, in the image of God created he him; male and female created he them."

When God said let us make man in our image, after our likeness, if we genuinely believe the scripture, we will be mindful how we speak not to pronounce negative words upon our life.

(4) Proverbs 18:21 "Death and life are in the power of the tongue: they that love it shall eat the fruit thereof."
(5) 1st kings 17:1 "And Elijah the Tishbite, who was of the inhabitants of Gilead, said unto Ahab, "As the Lord God of Israel lives, before whom I stand there shall not be dew nor rain there years, but according to my word."

(6) Luke 10:19 "Behold, I give unto you power to tread on serpents and scorpions and over all the power of the enemy and nothing shall by any means hurt you.

When we study the word of God, meditate on the word of God, believe the word of God, we will conquer the enemy. Look at the encounter of Jesus Christ when he fasted forty days and forty nights, (Matthew 4:1-11) the Bible tells us that Jesus was led up of the spirit into the wilderness to be tempted of the devil, Jesus overcame him by speaking the word.

When the dragon and his angels were cast out of Heaven, the power they had was not withdrawn. The enemy is still using the power to afflict, oppress, manipulate, hinder humanity. The enemy is still using evil words to pronounce evil upon destinies, marriages, careers, pregnancies, health. When the enemy is pronouncing evil words upon a life, conception or any area of life, you can reverse such words in Jesus name. As a young boy growing up in the family over fifty years ago, I witnessed the power of negative words spoken to my mother, as an only child of my mother. She had six miscarriages, and even had surgery with the hope that would solve the problem, however the surgery was not successful. There was a close relative who encouraged my father to marry another wife, saying my mother was a room and parlour, and they would give him another wife who would have children for him; this led to polygamy. Whilst my mother was looking for a solution to have another child, she was informed that her womb and personal wares were placed upon an evil altar, which was responsible for her having six miscarriages. The knowledge of God was not known to her. One of the chapters will be looking at the role of the evil altars. Some have experienced miscarriage, still birth, because of the negative spoken words over them, that they will never have children. In the years of praying with people believing God for the fruit of the womb, some have mentioned during the time of counselling, that they were told openly, as long they are alive, they will not have any children. The Bible tells us you shall decree a thing and it shall be established (Job 22:28). We have the assurance in the word of God, no matter the evil pronouncement of barrenness, it will be reversed in Jesus' name.

The following scriptures will reveal to us how it is possible for negative words to be released upon a destiny.

### Genesis 49:1-4:

1 "And Jacob called unto his sons, and said, gather yourselves together, that I may tell you that which shall befall you in the last days. 2 Gather yourselves together, and hear, ye sons of Jacob; and hearken unto Israel your father. 3 "Reuben, thou art my firstborn, my might, and the beginning of my strength, the excellency of dignity, and the excellency of power" 4"Unstable as water, thou shalt not excel; because thou wentest up to thy father's bed; then defiledst thou it: he went up to my couch."

### Exodus 1:15-16:

15 "And the king of Egypt spoke to the Hebrew midwives, of which the name of the one was Shiphrah, and the name of the other Puah":

16" And he said, when ye do the office of a midwife to the Hebrew women and see them upon the stools; if it be a son, then ye shall kill him: but if it be a daughter, then she shall live."

**Matthew 2:16:**

"Then Herod, when he saw that he was mocked of the wise men, was exceeding wroth, and sent forth, and slew all the children that were in Bethlehem, and in all the coasts thereof, from two years old and under, according to the time which he had diligently inquired of the wise men."

## Prayers: Dealing with Evil/Strange Words/Evil Decrees:

1. Every negative word I have spoken concerning my conception/pregnancy, be reversed by the Blood of Jesus Christ.
2. Every negative word of my father's house affecting my conception/pregnancy, be reversed by the blood of Jesus Christ.
3. Every negative word of my mother's house affecting my conception/pregnancy, be reversed by the blood of Jesus Christ.
4. Every negative word by my siblings affecting my conception/pregnancy, be reversed by the blood of Jesus Christ.
5. Every strange word by my in-laws affecting my conception/pregnancy, be reversed by the blood of Jesus Christ.

6. Every evil word spoken by strange kings/evil rulers from my place of birth affecting my divine conception/pregnancy, be reversed by the blood of Jesus Christ.
7. Every evil word spoken by wicked elders from my place of birth affecting my divine conception/pregnancy, be reversed by the blood of Jesus Christ.
8. Every evil decree placed upon my womb, be reversed by the blood of Jesus Christ.
9. Every decree of death placed upon my pregnancy, be challenged by fire.
10. Every word of miscarriage affecting my pregnancy, be reversed by the blood of Jesus Christ.
11. Every tongue anointed by Satan to hinder my pregnancy, I cut you off by the sword of Jehovah.
12. Every evil pronouncement waiting to manifest on my day of delivery, be consumed by fire.
13. Every evil decree waiting to manifest during my pregnancy, be consumed by fire.
14. Every vow placed upon my pregnancy, break in the name of Jesus Christ.
15. Every evil observer monitoring my pregnancy, be blinded by the blood of Jesus Christ.
16. Every serpent of my father's house, waiting to swallow my pregnancy, be consumed by fire.
17. Every serpent of my mother's house, waiting to swallow my pregnancy, be consumed by fire.
18. Every serpent of my in-law's house, waiting to swallow my pregnancy, be consumed by fire.
19. Every curse of still birth affecting my life, break, by fire.
20. Every curse of still birth affecting my life, break, by fire.

21. Every evil word spoken by any dead relative affecting my conception, be reversed, by the blood of Jesus Christ.
22. Every evil vow placed on my conception by any dead relative, be reversed, by the blood of Jesus Christ.
23. Father God let you word of fruitfulness manifest in Jesus's name.
24. Every negative word that has prospered in my life, let the effects and consequences be reversed by the blood of Jesus Christ.

# CHAPTER THREE

## THE ROLE OF EVIL ALTARS

### What is an Altar?

An Altar can be defined as a raised area in a house of worship. An Altar is the place where divinity meets man. An Altar is place of worship, it is a place of religious offerings, place of sacrifice, or used for other ritualistic purposes. The Altar signifies the place where God intervenes in one's life. According to scripture, Elkanah had two wives, they went to Shiloh yearly. He went there to worship the Lord and offer sacrifices to the Lord. The Bible tells us that Elkanah went yearly to Shiloh to seek the face of the Lord. *Trust the Lord that he would manifest his glory in your life.* Hannah made a vow to God, Samuel 1:11, ... and "she vowed a vow, and said, O lord of host, if thou wilt indeed look on the affliction of thine handmaid, but wilt give unto thy handmaid a man child, then I will give him unto the Lord all the days of his life, and there shall no razor come upon his head."

**Purpose of an Evil Altar:**

- A place of evil sacrifice.

- A place where lives / destinies are tied and bound.

- A place of satanic rituals.
- A place where destinies are destroyed.
- A place where wombs are tied and locked up.
- A place of bewitchment.
- A place of satanic delay.
- A place of enchantment.
- A place where a life can be afflicted.
- A place where a life can be terminated.
- A place where strange fire is ignited for destiny.

Let's Examine the following Scriptures:

**1. Genesis 22:9:**

"And they came to the place which God had told him of, and Abraham built an altar there, and laid wood in order, and bound Isaac his son, and laid him on the altar upon the wood."

Some lives, destinies, pregnancies, glory, career, marriages have been tied upon evil altars which are responsible for people experiencing, miscarriages, barrenness and hardship in various areas of life.

**2. Judges 6:25-30:**

"And it came to pass the same night, that the Lord said unto him, take thy fathers young bullock even the second bullock of seven years old, and throw down that altar of Baal that thy father hath, cut down the grove that is by it."

The evil altar of thy father's house such as the altar of Baal is responsible for misfortune in one's destiny.

### 3. 1st Samuel 28:1-11:

"Then said the woman whom shall I bring up unto thee? And he said bring me up Samuel."

According to the scripture names can be placed upon evil altars, things representing a life, destiny, personal garments can be place upon evil altars to cause misfortune, such as miscarriages and barrenness.

### 4. Numbers 23:1-2, 13-14, 27-30:

Balaam told Balak to build seven evil altars to enable him carry out his evil plot against Israel. Evil and wicked forces set up evil altars in families, villages, towns, cities, nations against the progress of God's people and God's work. Evil altars are responsible for tying down a destiny, placing a womb upon the altar, to ensure that the woman does not conceive. Most women will seek solutions medically, to ascertain why they cannot conceive. After going for various tests, they are informed nothing is wrong with them medically. It is just like the case in the Bible, the woman with the issue of blood for 12 years. The Bible informs us that she spent all that she had, yet had no solution.

I have come across families seeking the fruit of the womb who spent money on IVF, and it failed. To the glory of God, one of the families has testified that the Lord has blessed them with two children. One must have Faith and trust the Almighty God that he can bless every family seeking the fruit of the womb.

Looking at 1 Samuel 28:1-11, Scripture tells us, Saul was seeking a woman that had a familiar spirit. On getting to Endo, he was asked by the woman, "whom do you want me to bring up?" Saul answered by saying she should bring up Samuel.

My question to you: "What is upon the altar that is representing you?"

What is upon the altar affecting conception?
What is upon the altar affecting pregnancy?
What monetary value has been placed upon the altar to bring about barrenness?
How often is the altar receiving evil sacrifice to affect pregnancy?

I have heard of sanitary pads placed upon evil altars to make sure that conception is hindered. Evil altars must be destroyed in prayers to receive your deliverance and freedom.

### Prayers to Destroy Evil Altars:

1. Anything representing me on an evil altar catch fire.
2. Every evil altar bearing my name be consumed by fire.
3. Every altar of barrenness erected for my life, catch fire.
4. Every altar of miscarriage erected for my life, catch fire.
5. Every rope tying down my womb to an evil altar, catch fire.
6. Every rope tying down my pregnancy to an evil altar, catch fire.
7. Powers sitting upon my pregnancy on an evil altar, be unseated by fire.

8. Powers sitting upon my pregnancy on an evil altar, be unseated by fire.
9. Every altar receiving sacrifice concerning my life, fruit of the womb, catch fire.
10. Every altar regulating my cycle, be consumed my fire.
11. Every altar observing my womb, be blinded by the blood of Jesus Christ.
12. Every altar cursing my womb, be silenced by the fire of the Holy Ghost.
13. Every padlock used to lock my womb on the evil altar, be opened by the keys of fire. Matthew 16:19 "The scripture says behold I give unto you the keys of the kingdom, what ever you bind on earth is bound in heaven, what ever you loose on earth is loose in heaven."
14. Altars of my father's house speaking barrenness to my life, catch fire.
15. Altars of my mother's house speaking barrenness to my life, catch fire.
16. Altars of wicked elders speaking barrenness to my life, be consumed by fire.
17. Altars of my in laws house speaking barrenness to my life, catch fire.
18. Every evil priest in charge of an evil altar, I bind you, in Jesus' name.
19. Every strange fire ignited against my pregnancy, be consumed by fire.
20. Every padlock used to lock up my womb, and placed upon an altar, be opened by fire.

Spiritual Strategies to Combat Barrenness

# CHAPTER FOUR

## DISMANTLING THE ROLE OF WITCHCRAFT

**Exodus 22:18:**

"Thou shall not suffer a witch to live."

**Isaiah 49:26:**

"And I will feed them that oppress thee with their own flesh, and they shall be drunken with their own blood as with sweet wine and all flesh shall know that I the Lord am thy saviour and thy Redeemer, the mighty one of Jacob."

**Matthew 10:36:**

"And a man's foes shall be they of his own household."

**Micah 3:1-3:**

1. "And I said, Hear, I pray you, O heads of Jacob, and ye princes of the house of Israel; Is it not for you to know judgment?"
2. Who hate the good, and love the evil, who pluck off their skin from off them, and their flesh from off their bones.
3. Who also eat the flesh of my people and strip of their skin from off them; and they break their bones, and chop them in pieces, as for the pot, and as flesh within the caldron.

The scripture Micah 3:1-3 tells us the role of witchcraft, especially verse 3, tells us about witchcraft eating the flesh of the people, breaking bones, and chopping them in pieces and putting them in the pot. That's why witchcraft attacking conception, pregnancy must be confronted spiritually with acidic prayers. The Bible tells us in Matthew 11:12, "And from the days of John the Baptist until now the kingdom of heaven suffereth violence, and the violent take it by force."

From experience of counselling and praying with women seeking fruit of the womb some are not aware of the witchcraft powers dealing with them, or the witchcraft powers that are responsible for barrenness. There was a sister, while I was praying with her, the Lord revealed a family member vowed she would never have children. As a result of the revelation, I asked the lady certain questions, she revealed that she had two miscarriages and a still birth because of the evil pronouncement. To the glory of the Living God, the lady in question has two children.

Some have eaten the food of witchcraft, which is responsible for barrenness, some have eaten strange food in the dream, which can be responsible for barrenness. Some have eaten and drunken strange concoctions to help themselves, yet remain barren. One of the testifiers, testified they were given a strange concoction, but the problem persisted until they had a divine encounter.

Some have been under a spell of witchcraft, the witchcraft, being responsible for their barrenness, miscarriages and still birth. Some wombs had been placed upon witchcraft altars.

## Prayers: Dismantling Witchcraft Powers:.

1. Every altar of witchcraft responsible for barrenness in my life, catch fire..
2. Every witchcraft priest in charge of the altar of barrenness in my life, be bound by the chains of fire.
3. My womb tied to the altar of witchcraft, be loose by fire.
4. My organs tied to the altar of witchcraft be loose by fire.
5. Every spell of witchcraft upon my life, upon my womb, be consumed by fire.
6. Every evil mark placed upon my life, upon my womb, be blotted out by the blood of Jesus Christ.
7. Every food of witchcraft I have eaten, I vomit you out, by fire.
8. Every strange liquid I have consumed, be consumed by fire.
9. Every altar of witchcraft of my father's house responsible for barrenness, be consumed by fire.
10. Every altar of witchcraft of my mother's house responsible for barrenness, be consumed by fire.
11. Every altar of witchcraft of my in laws house, responsible for barrenness, catch fire.
12. Altar of wicked elders, speaking barrenness to my life, be consumed by fire.

13. Blood of Jesus Christ, purge my life, my womb, my fallopian tubes.
14. Blood of Jesus Christ minister healing to my organs.
15. Every witchcraft burial against my fruitfulness, be exhumed by fire.
16. Every witchcraft power that has swallowed my conception, vomit it by fire.
17. Every family serpent that has swallowed my pregnancy, vomit it by fire.
18. Every witchcraft mirror monitoring my life, break to pieces in Jesus' name.
19. Every witchcraft handwriting affecting my fruitfulness, be blotted out by the blood of Jesus Christ.
20. Garment of barrenness upon my life catch fire.
21. Garment of miscarriages upon my life catch fire.
22. Garment of still birth upon my life catch fire.
23. Every witchcraft curse affecting conception break by fire.
24. Every witchcraft control over my cycle, break by fire.
25. Every pot of witchcraft assigned against my pregnancy be consumed by fire.
26. Every caldron of witchcraft attacking my fruitfulness be consumed by fire.
28. Every caldron that hijacks my fruitfulness, release it by fire.
29. Every witchcraft that has prospered against me, let its effects and consequences be reversed by fire.
30. Holy Ghost overshadow me with your fire.

# CHAPTER FIVE
## DEALING WITH EVIL WEAPONS

### What is a weapon?

A Weapon can be defined as a knife, gun, club, which can be used to injure, defeat, or destroy, which has the capability to kill or cause serious injury to a person.

### Let's look at the following scriptures:

1. **Isaiah 54:17:** "No weapon that is formed the heritage of the servants of the Lord, and their righteousness is of me, saith the Lord.
2. **Psalm 91:5:** "Thou shall be afraid for the terror by night, nor for the arrow that flieth by day.
3. **Psalm 64:7:** "But God shall shoot at them with an arrow, suddenly shall they be wounded.

Weapons are used in combat, Nations use weapons to protect their territories, use weapons when at war. Likewise in the spiritual realm, weapons are being deployed in God's Kingdom and Satan's Kingdom. An example is the scripture of David and Goliath 1 Samuel 17:45:
"Then said David to the philistine, thou comest to me with a sword and with a spear, and with a shield, but I come to thee in the name of the Lord of Hosts, the God of the armies of Israel, whom thou have defiled. David had the faith to deal with the enemy.

Child of God, fear not, the Egyptians you see today, you shall see them no more in the name of Jesus Christ. The enemy uses the weapon of fear to harass people; bind the spirit of fear. Do not allow fear to become a stronghold in your life. According to scripture 2nd Corinthians 10:4, "For the weapons of our warfare are not canal, but mighty through God to the pulling down of strongholds."

There is a sister who belonged to the house fellowship of Arise and Shine. During the time of fellowship, the Lord revealed that her womb had holes in it. The womb was perforated. At that time, the sister was single. During the fellowship, the Lord revealed that he would seal up the holes. By the time the sister got married, the family were not expecting her to conceive, because in their generation it takes over 10 years for some of them to conceive. To the glory of God, the sister has three children within five years. The arrow that was responsible for the perforated womb, the Lord dealt with it during the time of fellowship. The sister in question has submitted her testimony which you will find in the testimony section of this book.

## Prayers Dealing With Evil Weapons:

1. Every evil arrow fired into my womb, jump out by fire.
2. Evil arrows targeting my pregnancy go back to sender.
3. Every evil arrow fired into my fallopian tube, jump out by fire.

4. Arrows of miscarriage fired into my life, jump out by fire.
5. Arrows of destruction fired into my womb jump out by fire.
6. Strange arrows in my body, womb, I shake you out by fire.
7. Arrows responsible for a leaking womb, jump out by fire.
8. Lord heal my womb with your fire.
9. Evil arrows waiting to be activated in my life/womb jump out by fire.
10. Evil arrows from my father's house responsible for barrenness jump out by fire.
11. Evil arrows from my mother's house responsible for barrenness jump out by fire.
12. Evil arrows of wicked elders from my place of birth, responsible for barrenness, jump out by fire.
13. Evil arrows programmed into my life, daily, monthly, yearly, return to sender.
14. Evil arrows targeting my pregnancy go back to sender.
15. Evil arrows waiting to be activated on the day of delivery, go back to sender.
16. Every tongue anointed by Satan to fire arrows, be cut off by the sword of Jehovah.
17. Every evil arrow that has prospered in my life, let their effects and consequences be reversed, by the blood of Jesus Christ.
18. Evil arrows fired to terminate pregnancy, go back to you sender.
19. Blood of Jesus Christ incubate my life.
20. Every embargo placed on my conception/pregnancy and my day of delivery, be consumed by the Holy Ghost fire in Jesus name.

**Spiritual Strategies to Combat Barrenness**

# CHAPTER SIX
## UPROOTING EVIL PLANTATIONS

**Matthew 15:13:** "But he answered and said, every plant which my heavenly father hath not planted, shall be rooted up."

**Matthew 13:25:** "But while men slept, his enemy came and sowed tares among the wheat, and went his way.

Some have eaten strange food physically or eaten food in the dream, which is responsible for barrenness.

One of the testifiers, testified during the period they were seeking for the fruit of the womb, the man mentioned he was given a concoction to drink which nearly killed him. He narrated the story after the Lord had blessed them with children. On narrating the story, we thought about the extent the devil can go to deceive people.

Some years ago, whilst praying with a sister trusting God for the fruit of the womb, the enemy brought food for her in the dream, to either cause her to miscarry or bring about pollution to the pregnancy at the time. At the time when the lady was having the dream the Lord was pressing it upon my spirit to call the sister, on calling the sister, she informed me that she was about eating the food, but the phone call woke her up, hence she did not eat the food. Some are poisoned physically; some eat strange food from the kingdom of darkness, prepared by satanic caterers which can impact conception and pregnancy.

The woman with the issue of blood, said to herself, if I touch the helm of his garment, I will be made whole, likewise the wicked one can touch a woman believing God for fruit of the womb to bring about barrenness, miscarriage, stillbirth, and delay.

A source of evil plantation, is the visit of a spirit husband in the dream which comes to defile the woman believing God for fruit of the womb. Plantation of fibroids can lead to loss of pregnancy during the first 23 weeks. There was a case of a sister who had multiple fibroids. She was informed by her Doctor it would be difficult to get pregnant unless the fibroids were surgically removed. This is one of the strategies the enemy uses by planting fibroids in a woman's life to hinder pregnancy.

The following scriptures give insight, because one needs to stand against evil plantations and evil visitations.

**Matthew 12:43-45:**

43 "When the unclean spirit is gone out of a man, he walketh through dry places, seeking rest, and findeth none.

44 Then he saith, I will return into my house from whence I came out; and when he is come, he findeth it empty, swept, and garnished.

45 Then goeth he, and taketh with himself seven other spirits more wicked than himself, and they enter in and dwell there: and the last state of that man is worse than the first. Even so shall it be also unto this wicked generation."

Looking at the scripture, one must stand against evil plantations and evil visitations. According to Matthew 12:44, "Then he saith, I will return into my house from whence I came out; and when he is come, he findeth it empty, swept, and garnished. As a child of God, one has to stand against this evil visitation and evil occupation of the enemy which acts as a stumbling block to being fruitful. One must block off the route they use to access one's life.

The enemy would give some Coca-Cola in the dream to drink, not knowing it is blood being consumed, thereby initiating one into witchcraft. The purpose of the enemy according to John 10:10 is this: "The thief cometh not, but to steal, and to kill, and to destroy."

According to the word of God in Matthew 15:13 "But he answered and said, every plant which my heavenly father hath not planted, shall be rooted out."

There is an assurance in the scripture, no matter how long an evil plantation has been there, it shall be uprooted, in Jesus' name. Child of God, be rest assured, the Earthquake of fire, the Consuming fire of God, shall consume every evil plantation in Jesus' name. Every Iroko tree, (strange tree), that needs to be consumed, shall be consumed, in Jesus' name. That is a word for someone.

## Prayers to Uproot Evil Plantations:

(1) Every tree of barrenness planted in my generation, be uprooted by fire.

(2) Every tree of barrenness in my life, be uprooted by fire.

(3) Every tree of miscarriage in my life, catch fire.

(4) Every tree of still birth in my life, be uprooted by fire.

(5) Every tree planted in my life to block pregnancy, catch fire.

(6) Every tree where my pregnancy has been suspended, catch fire.

(7) Every tree harbouring my pregnancy, I set you ablaze, by fire.

(8) Evil plantation troubling my destiny and conception,, catch fire and burn to ashes.

(9) Plantation of darkness in my life, catch fire.

(10) Plantation of darkness in my generation, catch fire.

(11) Plantation of darkness responsible for barrenness, miscarriage, still birth, catch fire and burn to ashes.

(12) Every plantation of fibroid, be consumed my the fire of the Holy Ghost

(13) Every tree in my father's/mother's house responsible for barrenness, miscarriage and still birth in my life, catch fire in Jesus' name.

(14) Every strange drink/concoction that I have drunk physically or in a dream, I vomit you out by fire, in Jesus' name.

(15) Blood of Jesus Christ, purge my life.

(16) Blood of Jesus Christ, close every route the enemy is using to access my life.

(17) Every evil occupation of the enemy in my life, be chased out by fire.

(18) Every evil occupation of the enemy in my womb, come out by fire.

(19) Every stronghold of wickedness occupying my life, be chased out by fire.

(20) Powers in charge of evil plantation in my life, be bound in Jesus' name.

**Spiritual Strategies to Combat Barrenness**

# CHAPTER SEVEN

## DELIVERANCE FROM SPIRITUAL PRISONS:

### What is a Prison?

According to the English dictionary, a Prison is a building in which people are legally held as a punishment for a crime they have committed. It is a correctional facility, a detention centre.

### Characteristics of a Prison:

- It is place of solitary confinement.
- It a place under lock and key.
- It a place guarded by security officers.
- It a place where lives are bound with chains.
- It is place of loneliness and frustration.
- It a place where a destiny can be sentenced to life. An example was late Nelson Mandela who spent 27 years in prison in South Africa.
- According to Mark 3:27, the prison is the place where the enemy stores goods belonging to the children of God.

> The enemy has placed a lot of destinies, conceptions, and pregnancies in spiritual prisons. While praying with a couple, the Lord showed me spiritual warehouses where unborn babies had been stored. It will take the divine intervention of God for people who find themselves in such predicaments to be set free. The enemy can place a man in a spiritual prison, which would make it difficult for the couple to conceive.

When we look at the story of Daniel, where he fasted for 21 days, the Bible tells us that the prince of Persia withheld the angel bringing the answers to his prayer for 21 days until reinforcement was dispatched from Heaven. Likewise, a lot of people believing God for fruit of the womb might find themselves in such a predicament, where the Angel bringing the answers to their prayers are hijacked.

The scripture tells us Paul and Silas were placed in the prison. Likewise, a lot of destinies, pregnancies and unborn babies have been placed in spiritual prisons. Powers of thy father's house can sentence a destiny to spiritual prison to cause frustration, stagnation and delay.

Let's look at the following scriptures!

Mark 3:27: "No man can enter into a strong man's house and spoil his goods, except he will first bind the strongman, and then he will spoil his house."

Acts 16:16-26 (v23) And when they had laid many stripes upon them, they cast them into prison, charging the jailer to keep them safely."

The scripture tells us Paul and Silas were placed in the prison. Likewise, a lot of destinies, pregnancies, unborn babies have been placed in spiritual prisons. It will take the Almighty God to reveal where pregnancies and unborn babies have been locked up in spiritual prisons.

## Where you will find a Spiritual Prison:

- In the grave (Ezekiel 37: 12-14.
- In the body of the waters (Jeremiah 46:8).
- In the belly of Leviathan (Psalm 74:14).
- A spiritual store house of the enemy )Mark 3:27).
- The second Heaven.

## How to get out of the Spiritual Prison:

1. Bind the strongman in charge of the prison according to scripture, in **Mark 3:27.**

2. Use the keys of the kingdom of God. Matthew 16:19 "And I will give unto thee the keys of the kingdom of heaven: and whatsoever thou shalt bind on earth shall be bound in heaven: and whatsoever thou shalt loose on earth shall be loosed in heaven."

3. **1 Thessalonians 5:17,** "Pray without ceasing." Paul and Silas when they were put in prison prayed (Act 16:25), "And at midnight Paul and Silas prayed and sang praises unto God: and the prisoners heard them."

4. Prayer of authority: Come forth. **John 11:41-43.**

Jesus demonstrated the prayer of authority in **John 11:41-43,** v 43 "And when he thus had spoken, he cried with a loud voice, Lazarus come forth.

You can call forth every pregnancy that had been locked in the spiritual prison, in the body of the waters, in the grave, spiritual store houses and in the second heaven.

5. Command every grave housing my pregnancy, fruitfulness to be opened by fire.

### Ezekiel 37:12-14:

12 "Therefore prophesy and say unto them, thus saith the Lord God; Behold, O my people, I will open your graves, and cause you to come up out of your graves, and bring you into the land of Israel.

13 And ye shall know that I am the Lord, when I have opened your graves, O my people, and brought you up out of your graves,

14 And I shall put my spirit in you, and ye shall live, and I shall place you in your own land: then shall ye know that I the Lord have spoken it, and performed it, saith the Lord."

(6) Command the strange clothing to be burnt.

### John 11:44:

"And he that was dead came forth, bound hand and foot with grave clothes: and his face was bound about with a napkin. Jesus saith unto them, loose him, and let him go."

When people are sentenced to prison, they put on prison clothes for the duration of their sentence. Like wise any thing the enemy has stolen and put in spiritual prison, would be covered with strange clothing.

### Deliverance prayers from Spiritual Prison:

**(1) Binding the strongman: Mark 3:27**

- Every strongman in charge of any prison in the body of the waters housing my conception; pregnancy, be bound in Jesus' name.
- Every strongman of my in laws that has hijacked my conception, pregnancy be bound in Jesus' name.
- Every strongman sitting upon my fruit of the womb, I bind you and unseat you by fire.

## (2) Command the Prison gates/doors to be opened: Matthew 16:19

- Every spiritual prison housing the fruit of my womb, be opened by fire.
- Every spiritual prison in the body of the water, be opened by the seaquake of the Lord.
- Every grave housing my conception and pregnancy, be opened by fire.
- Every forest housing the fruit of my womb, release it by fire.
- Every spiritual prison in the second heaven housing my fruitfulness, be opened by fire.
- Every spiritual prison in my father's house, housing the fruit of my womb, be opened by fire.
- Every spiritual prison in my mother's house, housing the fruit of my womb, be opened by fire.
- Every spiritual prison in my in laws house, that is housing the fruit of my womb, be opened by fire.
- Every serpent of my father's house that has swallowed the fruit of my womb, vomit it by fire.
- Every serpent of my mother's house that has swallowed the fruit of my womb, vomit it by fire.
- Every serpent of my in laws house that swallowed the fruit of my womb, vomit it by fire.

### (3) Come forth by Fire: John 11:41-43

- Every spiritual prison housing the fruit of my womb, come forth by fire.
- Every spiritual prison in the second heaven housing the fruit of my womb, come forth by fire.
- Every spiritual prison in the body of the waters housing the fruit of my womb, come forth my fire.
- Every grave housing the fruit of my womb, come forth by fire.
- Every prison in my father's house, housing the fruit of my womb, come forth by fire.
- Every prison in my mother's house, housing the fruit of the womb, come forth by fire.
- Every prison in my in laws house, housing the fruit of the womb, come forth by fire.
- Every strange covering used to cover my conception and pregnancy in the realm of the spirit, be consumed my fire.
- Every strange covering used to cover my conception and pregnancy in the body of the waters, be consumed by fire.
- Every strange covering, used to cover my conception and pregnancy in the forest, be consumed by the consuming fire of God.
- Every strange covering used to cover my conception and pregnancy in my father's house, be roasted to ashes.
- Every strange covering, used to cover my conception and pregnancy in my mother's house, be consumed by Fire.

## (4) Strange covering to be consumed by fire:

- Every strange clothing from the grave, used to cover my conception and pregnancy, be consumed by fire.
- Every strange covering used to cover my conception and pregnancy, in the body of the waters, be consumed by fire.
- Every strange covering used to cover my conception and pregnancy in the forest, be consumed by the consuming fire of God.
- Every strange covering used to cover my conception and pregnancy in my father's house, be roasted to ashes.
- Every strange covering used to cover my conception and pregnancy in my mother's house, be consumed by Fire.
- Every strange covering used to cover my conception and pregnancy in my mother's house, burn to ashes.
- Every strange clothing from the grave used to cover my conception and pregnancy, be consumed by fire.

# TESTIMONIES

## Testimony 1

I am sister Florence by name, I had been waiting on the Lord for the fruit of the womb for a period of five years. In that period of waiting, I had two miscarriages and a still birth. After persistent prayers, I was told my prayer had been answered, but while waiting for the manifestation, I told God to confirm it for me through another person. To the glory of God, I met Pastor Chiduzie who came for a program in Lagos (Nigeria) 2014. On that faithful day we met at the reception office, he looked at me and said I can see a baby, you are carrying a baby, and I narrated how I had been believing God on issues of child bearing and he started praying with me before he left for the United Kingdom. Shortly after a month, that he left for the U.K, I conceived and he was praying with me, till I delivered my baby. I thank God for sending Pastor to me during my waiting period. When I delivered my baby in 2015, I was so happy, on the eight day, for the baby to be named. Pastor called and gave a word that I would be having another baby. I said no, "let the baby I have be grown first." By the time I knew it, I was pregnant again, and to the glory of God, I had two children within two years.

*Praise God. Sis Florence (Nigeria).*

## Testimony 2

Praise be to God for his mercy endures forever. I have been a member of Arise and Shine house fellowship for over 10 years Through this ministry, headed by Pastor Chiduzie Nmecha, the Almighty God blessed my family tremendously when all hope had faded. We prayed for my daughter who had a series of miscarriages and by the help of God, who answered prayers by fire and consistent prayer support from Pastor Chiduzie Nmecha, God heard our cries, wiped away our tears and blessed my daughter with three beautiful children.

Psalm 120:1, In my distress I called to the Lord, and he answered my prayer.

Thank you, Pastor Chidi, for your unwavering prayer support. May the Almighty God continue to use you mightily and may his anointing on your head overflow for the work you are doing for people in Jesus' name. To the glory of God, I have five grandchildren.

*Sister Adoley Laryea.*

## Testimony 3

Yoke of Barrenness Broken with Divinely Inspired Prayers:

A Pastor and his wife had been married for six years, and had tried IVF, which turned out to be very risky, and eventually was not successful.

But during fervent and consistent family prayers which began after February 2017, the Lord began to reveal foundational structures, (polygamy, rituals, idolatry), which were responsible for the delay, as well as the current household enemy perpetuating it. The Lord cut off their evil control, stopped the household enemy having further physical contact with them, till date.

The strongholds were broken by divine direction in prayers, and they had their first baby in 2018, on the 7th anniversary of their wedding, and the second one followed swiftly, in 2020, all to the glory of God.

*Pastor Ike (Nigeria).*

## Testimony 4

A Pastor friend of mine who went to see a Couple:

"I went to see a couple who were looking for the fruit of the womb, a quarrel ensued between them. I tried as much as I could to settle the quarrel and left their house.

A call came in from my friend and brother a man of God. I told him the story of the couple, and he quickly said, "I saw a baby coming," which I shared with the couple. That same month, the sister took in, but miscarried. I shared with the man of God Pastor Chiduzie and he assured me that God will do as he said. She eventually took in again a few months afterwards and a had a baby girl."

*Pastor Chidi (UK).*

## Testimony 5

My wife and I had been believing God for the fruit of the womb after few years of marriage. Due to the challenges, we were experiencing, we considered ending the marriage. During this waiting period, we came to know Pastor Chiduzie, who took it as a burden upon himself to always pray with us. Pastor and his family have been good family prayer partners, as God has been using Pastor in the place of prayer, visits, calls, among others. One faithful morning, my wife complained about stomach pain which took her to hospital for medical intervention. It was then made known to us that she was pregnant. Along with the pregnancy, complications almost made us lose hope, which we related to Pastor who encouraged and continued to pray with us. Finally, to God be the glory, we had the first baby with joy and gladness. When our first baby was born, we invited Pastor to the naming ceremony. When Pastor prayed for the baby, he prayed that when the baby would be a year old, we would come back for the arrival of the second baby.

When the baby was a year old, we invited Pastor and there was the arrival of the second baby, as he prayed in the previous years. When Pastor arrived, he said, "can he prophesy?" We said no, but to our surprise, we had three children within five years. Thanks be to God Almighty for using Pastor as a tool to bless my family.

*Brother and Sister in Christ.*

## Testimony 6

My name is Okolo Obiora from Enugu state in Nigeria, I got married on the 12th of September 2009, I was a Banker; I love my wife very much and she is very beautiful and dedicated to God. We started living together and hoping that one day she will take in and we will have a baby. She had miscarriages and she cried, but I consoled her and said that we should wait on the Lord, even some of my friends started telling me that I should get another woman to marry. Some said that I should go outside and get another woman pregnant and bring her into my home, but thank God for my relations, especially my mum, she is a mother and she equally believes in God greatly. She always advised us that with God, all things are possible. Then her sister had the same experience, and she overcame it, and everything was settled. My own case would not be different. I met Pastor Chiduzie when he came to Nigeria in 2014. He was praying with people and I narrated my story to him. He continued to pray with us, even when he went back to the United Kingdom. In the year 2017, towards the last two months, the Lord visited us. My wife gave birth on 23rd July, 2018 to a beautiful baby girl, her name is Chizaram Favour Okolo. She is very sound and intelligent; I thank God for His faithfulness and blessings. I and my wife, Mrs Prisca Ngozi Okolo, will ever be grateful to God Almighty, in Jesus' name.

*Okolo Obiora.*

## Testimony 7

Our paths crossed for a reason...

Pastor Chiduzie has been a blessing to me and my family. I met him 19 years ago while still a student and single. I plaited his daughter's hair every month, but I never knew he would become family I could count on. When I finished University, I was looking for a job. He saw me and told me that I would get a job soon. And that happened, just as he prophesied. I thought it was just a one-off prophecy, but I didn't know that there were more to come.

A few years later, I decided to join their house fellowship group and Pastor Chiduzie was the house fellowship leader. There was a day God showed him that my womb was leaking blood. He prayed with me and told me that God had performed a miracle in my womb.

A couple of years later, I met my husband, and he continued to pray for me for the fruit of the womb. Every time we prayed; God showed signs of celebration. One day, I went to their house for fellowship. He looked at me and laughed. I asked him why he was laughing. He said that he was seeing a baby crawling next to me. The next day, I felt a sharp pain in my stomach. When I went to the hospital, they told me that I was pregnant. I was not aware I was pregnant, when the Hospital told me I was pregnant. I then remembered what Pastor said to me the previous day.

Today, I am a mother of three children. Only God can do this. I cannot forget what God has done for me through his vessel, Pastor Chiduzie.

*Sister Nikki (France).*

## Testimony 8

The journey in testifying to the glory of God Almighty in the life of Pastor Chiduzie started in 1999, when we started attending a church fellowship in London. Prior to this time, we had experienced a couple of un-explained pregnancy miscarriages. It would happen each time after 20-weeks. These mis-carriages extremely surprised and baffled medical consultants at Kings College Hospital London.

When we started attending the Church fellowship, we also met couples experiencing the same life situation as ourselves, and which ultimately encouraged, motivated, and inspired us that we were not alone in this challenging situation. It wasn't long after our first few months of attending the fellowship, that we realised, that the situation was more a spiritual one, than that of a medical one. We were enlightened after couples who had experienced the same situation shared their testimonies. This emboldened, encouraged and drove us to be more committed to a relationship with God instead.

Pastor Chiduzie, coming from a medical background, sharing his own life testimony and as one of the Pastors in charge of the fellowship group - "Looking for Fruit of the Womb" (LFW), was assigned to us. This opened-up for us, a personal, family and spiritual relationship, that led to a life changing and transforming process, by the mighty hand of God Almighty.

Pastor Chiduzie personally - and some few other pastors - took that personal interest and charge; prayed that through the fervent prayers of the righteous, the name of God Almighty will be glorified and testified to, in the mighty name of our Lord Jesus Christ. Thus, the process to pray, day and night, for God Almighty to intervene, and take total and absolute control of every situation challenging our conception battle, was generated.

After months of relentless prayers day and night prayers, fasting and deliverance, going through the process with Pastor Chiduzie: calling to pray with my wife every morning and evening and constantly checking up on the general well-being of her situation, she eventually conceived again. The battle and challenge to carry the pregnancy all the way through the nine-month cycle, was another chapter of life experience.

It was one battle to another, leading to many Hospital admissions, without any specific reason. But, by this time, God Almighty had shown his mighty hand and shewn forth great knowledge as to why this battle had to manifest with many prayers.

We had victory to his Holy and Mighty name. God Almighty is more than able to make the impossible – possible. After months of relentless prayer battles with Pastor Chiduzie and other Pastors standing in the gap, we had victory. They interceded with aggressive prayer sessions, counselling, supporting, and inspiring us from time to time.

My wife gave birth, to the victory and testimony, that God Almighty rules in the affairs of men, to the glory of his Holy and Mighty name. I testify to the strength and power of God Almighty, to overcome every battle that confronts, challenges or wants to hinder the glory of the work of His hands, in the life of his children.

From the parents of wonderful children. To God Almighty be the glory of His name.

*Mr & Mrs Obikoya London (UK).*

www.ingramcontent.com/pod-product-compliance
Lightning Source LLC
LaVergne TN
LVHW011413080426
835511LV00005B/520